Connoisseur

Dawn Wood

Templar Poetry

First Published 2009 by Templar Poetry
Templar Poetry is an imprint of Delamide & Bell

Fenelon House
Kingsbridge Terrace
58 Dale Road, Matlock, Derbyshire
DE4 3NB
www.templarpoetry.co.uk

ISBN 978-1-906285098

A CIP catalogue record of this book is available from the British Library.

Typeset by Pliny
Graphics by Paloma Violet
Printed and bound in India

With thanks to all at the Barrack Street Museum, Dundee

Acknowledgements

Thanks are due to the editors of Magma, and Poetry Ireland Review, in which some of these poems first appeared. Forbes' *de rerum natura* is based on an exhibition by artist Ronald Forbes.

Contents

Eileen photographs a piece of whale curated for the new mc manus galleries

The wages on *The Dorothy* include halfpennies.
There are harpooners, seamen, a surgeon.
They are paid a deposit and then, in oil.
In handwriting, in 1829, in exquisite,
exquisite handwriting, the seafarers sign
that they have received their money,
or in broad ink swirls, or someone signs,
squint across the tissue-pink rules, for them.
We are so crude, we have regressed,
if this is anything to judge by. *The Dorothy*
would have been as spindly as *The Discovery*;
the men, disembarked, would have been
kitchen-sink dancers against the snow,
but hungry, at work, tapered hands tending
the museum of the whale bones white.
The Captain would have kept his *Remarke Book*
updated with comet sightings, for example.
One glass negative has been wrongly captioned:
Fishing at the Mouth of the Jordan, Northern Galilee.

Surgo

A pond skater might innocently park
the floating spark of itself on the material surface,
but it knows well, below the swan-disruption
of fish past, or the while before dive
of a fisher-bird, echoed in the medium,
or current, the surge and dunt of spring
and that ice upstream clinging to dear hope.

My wave thoughts are that a mouse's song
is not in actual fact beyond hearing,
but a swooping flute of chirrups and whistles,
rare as a halo to hear it, but you could delve tomorrow
and find it no discrete sawn form but particles and springs
already quiver-ful since sound might be as sensitive

as you or me. A dunt of atoms makes a wave but
words go with the wind, and dunts are of the devil
as well as something that is felt by the heart,
just as the medium made me feel an accordion
at my heels, since she said the man was already
in the room, shouldering little lambing hands.

Spring and it is as rare as a halo to be condensed,
to float a spell between extremes
to part and parcel the punched-lettered lattice

of how we got from here to here, when the waves
closed our eyes. Were we talking little things,
were we asleep, before we met?

Was it simply when it happened, receipt?
My thoughts, on reading of the ultrasonic sounds of mice:
that the mouse's song is not beyond sound
and it can be slowed or the pitch shifted –
the mouse sings as a swooping flute, it whistles,
it chirrups. I do not think that anything is ever,
at the base-line, really silent.

Thus, nine ways of waving

Thank-you
for your animated dunt
of particles and springs.

Thank-you for your dunt
to particles on springs
which are animated.

Animation
is a spring of dunts
amongst particles.

The particles and springs
dunt you
thanks, animatedly.

Spring particles are animated
with the dunt
of my thanks.

A particle of thanks
spring-dunts
you, in animation.

A thank-you is a particle
springing with
animated dunts.

A dunt is an animated
thank-you
of particulate spring.

Spring
is particles and dunt
belatedly thanking you.

Swift

Not to be flippant, but not a *say less* bird
his Jonah's whale of a mouth opens
again the opening of itself.

He can ball his throat, should he collect enough
to not store, and his upper mandible
is more narwhal.

Brows down and glossy back, with his insect diet,
his walking sideways mites are hidden.

Mad. If he lands, he's doomed.

Simulacra

Is it not a wonder
that we don't trip over
or batter into them?
Or sail them like kites
or bail them as harvests
or braid them as Medusa worms
around our albino heads.
They float off, exogenously,
integral only to light,
finding the right verb
to turn live to love,
to be those unfurling
strands from incense.

Bedeviled

When I sketch 'x', say, a little owl,
I see that all my colleagues at tea-break
are devouring their elevenses with sickle beaks,
that they have urgent, full-moon eyes.

A little owl has sequestered my looking:
I realise that little owl traits are possible,
dispersed and spirited below
the mask of everyone.

My little owl is a Venus Fly Trap,
he is a hooded red riding hood,
he is innocent but he is innocence
bonneted and cloaked;

I have looked too much and I am hooked.
He is making me make light of him
so that I can draw him, tightly in
the down-stroke of a night feather.

One attribute of nature, then,
is Little Owlness. But there is a rolling
storage system there are shelves of this stuff.
It will be a long night, by the look of things.

Eclipse of the northern white rhino in charcoal

They say that the birds would have stopped singing,
though the clouds of midges didn't ease,
nor, I suppose did the tide's slow wash
over the succulent plants used to brine,
but Achill was a brave place for the eclipse
and our old lives were consumed as we watched
that velvet moon and mist shield us
as if we'd seen a child held over the cliff edge
and there had been sharks below, as indeed
he did and there were, though it was not yet
my own child, decorated with red flowers
as the sheep are painted in primaries
on that island for their owners. Great, careless
Irish splodges, all solid as a sun remains.

The Northern White Rhino bides his time
on the front of a notebook. Like the rooks
in the Georgics, he is not able to predict
the future, but he knows from the weather,
that something rare has been condensed
and that it is not as it was before, when the wind
was herding the clouds, but, instead, a wakening
as sweet as moss-scented air will happen,
a mouth will open, he will become a metaphor
for coming to terms with things – he is a seal, a branch,

a promise. In which case, hoards of the Northern White
are up and running, a sunrise of rhinos
after an eclipse – final animals cloned and cloven.
Wood turned to coal is the best medium.

In the museum of things against entropy

there is a child who says: mummy,
what happens your brain when you die?
Look, she replies, at that golden marmoset,
how its hair feathers, like a sea anemone;
see how its fingers grasp something
missing, a clarinet perhaps. And the child sees
that it could not ever have been a clarinet,
and yet the monkey looks, for all the world,
as if it is playing an absent clarinet.

They turn to see bones, labelled
and exploded on card, white against blue,
an alien set of Jack-straws pieces, neither
hoe, ladder, scythe, nor piccolo, nor flute.
Here is one articulation of a live thing –
that, for a while, it does its utmost
to furl and feather the gist of itself
against disorder; it will dart and deuk
into the white shell or star that it is.

The mother does not show the child
the incendiary colours of the sunbirds
and the hummingbirds, as mad as peacocks,
though they are stored, close by, in cabinets,
which anyone could open, without a care

in the world, except the one thought,
if they took the time to dwell on it, that this
fluttering, curious movement – hand to touch –
was conscious, in a nutshell, separate from the music.

From Forbes' *de rerum natura*

In the quest for knowledge, squirrels' pouched paws
hooked on to pollen make the devils' own work;
jerry-work hems, not in the same league of ruby,
make the angels', whose swift wings switch
and ruffle to coat a bucky-ball of their own alternate flour.
Incompatible as brandy-boilings and marbles,
there are enough worlds to go round, each mouth
sieving its element, hungry for the absence of purity.
That swallowed grit easily cradles the gooseberry bush
that gives rise to a monstrous pearl or a rose.

Mercury, however, follows his nose, snap-shots
of where he was at his heels and the look of budgerigars –
who'd buy a book of Peters and Pauls caged?
Is he the god who doffs his bowler to grant
parking-spaces and cancellations? Certainly,
at his behest, luddites avoiding meetings bow
to blow blackberries at diligent attendees,
though strains of *seas run dry* will never threaten
that wickedly happy maverick playing
his murder-winking game – has he ripped
the smiles from those upper angels to ruche his boots,
or are they giving him gyp, being his powdery parasites?
Herculean advocate, his is the message to change things.

Colony

The basking seals' equivalent of chess –
the seeming mystery
of who is given at any one time
to roll, wallow, nudge;

in which order the juveniles race,
and which piebald others turn to watch –
their Persian carpet coats
so many knots to the inch;

the mosaic of the ones that will scurry
to a new position –
they are the whiskered silverfish
of the breakfast-room floor of the ocean –

and the motionless, lined-up-to-dry
sea-urchin shells, bleached, spared
puff-ball fungi, shielded
by the interested dog's heads that patrol –

their bow of sand
is the ridge of the ear
of the Saint Bernard that is, himself,
the ear of the terrier of the Fife coastline.

Reassurance, also
the isolated orphan
with a matt gleam in his eyes,
his kin are making the whoop and ease

of the wind in the rigging,
the wuthering in the pines,
adopted by skylarks,
then by the Tentsmuir-accented chaffinch.

When your time is up, your time is up,
the wisest of the people used to forecast.
And when it's not, its not.

Eurydice, additional version

It is a strange gift, to see your own face
as it will look, when it is decaying,
to feel how it will disintegrate –
every hair, a night sentinel,
every cell, a volcano of self destruction;
to know your heart beat ease

and, no, your life will not flash before your eyes;
you will only think: how amazing the body is.
You will call it 'the body' to yourself,
now that you know it to be wilful,
desiring, in its own way,
what must happen.

It will also be a gift to see your face regain
its hollows and curves, as he walks
resolutely up the garden path,
to where you have been waiting,
you having been the one to lead the way
and without that glance back taken.

A be'ed a

A be'ed a is an expression used in Ulster Irish –
it means, roughly, I'd better,
but more than that:
it would be decent to,
it would be almost unthinkable not to.

People would notice, if you didn't.
For example if a person is in hospital,
it goes without saying that you'd visit,
but *a be'ed a bring grapes*
is what you would say to yourself.

If I have to give up my allotment
and move what matters to my new plot,
I'd want to take the apple trees I set
when I was a novice, and pruned
the plum branchless.

But a be'ed a leave them,
the *James Grieve*, the *Howgate Wonder*
as a gesture for the new tender,
who may, when I'm gone,
raise everything to the ground.

Maisie once grabbed the only apple,

without thinking, as she skipped past
the neighbour's garden. He stormed
to the door, but, when she said sorry,
he shook her hand.

In Ireland, we'd have said:
she be'ed a apologise and he'd
have nodded curtly when she did.
And the apple would have tasted
quite the contrary from what she'd expected.

Pure

This is why I don't quite believe
in equations. Haven't you noticed
how the pattern hovers over the surface,

so that it is not simply a rule
of one motif to one featherlet, hook or barb,
say, in the barn owl.

Look at him, gowned,
almost wearing ermine, but rather
than the soft shell of him being dotted

with stitches, or marks
where the tails used to be,
there are kohl-rimmed, almond eyes on him –

he has been branded *mine* by Isis
who says: slate clean, if you love me,
and his real eyes are pools of *I do*.

He is a go-between, the envoy of an instant
dappled with late sunlight
and then the white sheet of him

drawn swiftly upwards
through water, blotted to be born,
stung with eyes that never sleep

on the back of his head.
He hears with most of his face.
You could not startle such a being.

Bear

Christ Almighty! – Mike – *this thing's alive!*
Twitching! She's going to wake and see herself flayed
on her ventral surface, skin and fatty layers
gone. *It'll be the salt* – Joe was calm, claims
he's forgotten the incident, or was he, by then,
half way up the Hilltown, Beano-style puffs
at his heels? Mike, taxidermist, white as a sheet,
did his best to finish the skinning of Jemima,
who'd bitten the hand of a trespassing youth,
though her days were genuinely done,
and a new breeding pair had been brought along
to the children's zoo at Camperdown.
Mind you, he hasn't seen any pictures
of a sugar-puff cub in *The Courier* since.

He sent her skin to a tanner. Horror:
he opened the box and she'd come back
a rug, the crucial bits of her jowl cut off.
He made the best of the botched job –
chopped her into a joke wig, a sporran,
thought: too moth eaten for a car-seat cover.
Her bones were stored at Christian Salvesen,
a frozen food company on the Kingsway,
along with a couple of seals and a puffin.
In the eighties, Mike used to visit, to check

the museum's pallet. The last time,
surprised, he rummaged out a great lump,
thrown in with the samples – not a piece
of Jemima, but freezer-burnt, pilfered bacon.

Word of mouth on the taxidermy grapevine:
a cull happening, of bears, in Finland. So,
a replacement Jemima was commissioned,
to demonstrate the fauna of prehistoric Scotland.
Her skin is plush, fitted round a sculptured,
light as a feather, polystyrene core. She extends a paw:
she will not devour any visitor or trespasser
or fellow exhibits, except in the universes
of the night, where she gobbles the whole caboodle,
and sets off, a Bruno of a troubadour,
red hanky on a bony stick; her face,
the crested mask of a feral Helios; her eyes,
not the cross-stitch winks of teddies, but buttoned,
inscrutable, having abandoned all ties.

Her grace

There was no end to her grace –
it was as indefinite as that tissue paper Bible,
when she would lick her fingers
and riffle past salmon edges and copious annotations,
to reach some apt text, or other;

her grace was as luxurious in taking its time,
as her hand with the special tweezers,
poised like a budgerigar, over the fluted Chinese box
on her dressing table, to peck
the scrolled up message of the day;

she was praying in that spontaneous, Protestant way,
but struggling for a word, and the whole enterprise
was redundant anyway, because she was sneakily
wolfing down her leg of lamb, with her eyes
half-closed, and half-amber on the central platter.

I was the only one playing the waiting game.
Seated to my left, my sister, the one who's taro card
said *find out who you are meant to be!*
try on the world's hats! suggested
between mouthfuls – do you mean *nurturing*?

and our mother nodded, munching happily,
starting to stutter the gleeful pantomime of the next word.
I knew I'd have to yield again until she bailed me out,
so I cut the cord, and woke as hungry
as the flame below a red hot-air balloon.

Viscous

Stern men used to tell us in sermons
about the Greek word for love,
they'd have been advocating *agape*,
not fleeting *eros*.

That fish is the reason
I first turned to *fickle* in the dictionary.
Fortune must be a smiling sort:
how well trained is her naked fish!

Stubborn, it takes its turn to lie,
flat-footed in all of our palms.
We know that Fortune is not that rigid,
she has jealousy, and passion,

and distraction, in her bag of tricks.
If the fish had been still
in just one of our palms,
then we'd have understood.

A teatowel for Stuart

The ghosts thought that you'd like, for your birthday,
a tea-towel, with two lobsters printed on it.
I got it at Liberties, when I was in London.
It is fine linen and was a ridiculous price for a tea-towel,
but they made me queue to buy it.

I put it under my coffee table and forgot it was there,
until a month or so before your birthday,
when they made you shout very loudly,
in a lull in the conversation after evensong,
TWO LOBSTERS!

Remember, we called you over and said –
this is proof of our conversation,
that you interrupted, about time and life's events
and you looked a bit worried, and we laughed,
all will be revealed on the 6th of November.

The choice had been either a green cabbage,
or a Victorian domed jelly from a mould,
but I'd thought to myself, two lobsters
are better than one. It is too good to use,
you should frame it for display.

It is not for drying dishes.
It is a Wisdom of Solomon tea-towel,
evidence of something about time,
and life's events and the phantoms
that wiggle your tongue, and make my decisions.

Charm

A Buff-winged Starfrontlet
and a White-vented Amazilia
were stuck in a vent. Said the Amazilia
to the Frontlet: *I'm a little hunchbacked.*
Said the Frontlet: *please, not buff,*
there are elephants of iridescence
yet to be mentioned.

A White-chinned Sapphire and a Sunbird
were trapped in the mud.
Said the Yellow-bellied Sunbird:
your chin has discoloured.
Said the Sapphire: *with your colour,*
you must really like butter,
let us wallow as pigs in clover.

A Vermillion Flycatcher and a million
other hummingbirds were in a spot of bother.
I've got fire on the brain, whispered
Venus' little whiskered tongue.
Between us species, said the Violet Ear,
where white is, is what differs,
nor smiles any ear but your own.

Merlin

for Mike Nicholl

The school kids are bound to ask
why does that bird have a lollipop stick up it's bum?
But that's how he arranges the skins
these days, streamlined for handling
and storage, not in obvious poses

though he could make a robin sing,
in fact it might be harder not to,
their form flexes so easily that way –
it's what they do – if they're not fighting,
they're singing.

He blow-dries the back of the merlin's head,
which is almost bald,
to a salt-and-pepper effect.
The quill-pins are sheathed, blue-black
with blood, where the feathers would have grown.

The legs and feet are swollen, sticky
with bruising. It was trampled,
perhaps by a deer.
Each claw curves into half
that symbol of wholeness.

And the merlin chick is as good
it's going to get:
he thinks he got away with it –
twelve days old, but pretty ropy,
Ode to Joy, under-rehearsed, conductor on holiday.

Connoisseur

The sign of a brave man
is not that he has inherited many things,
or rejected them, in order that he might pass
though the eye of a needle.

The sign of a man of thought
is not that he announces that he cares for nothing,
as he shows his hands to be as empty of objects
as those of the Buddha of Compassion

no: he is willing to become another man
and he is as mystified as any
who have been called to bathe
in their hometown rivers.

The sign of clean water is not the mass of bees
that are working the overhanging foliage,
nor the many creatures with tails and eyes
that have been dredged from mire.

Clarity is a needle, threaded through with possibilities;
a tightrope, on which slip past
the one trick pony, the one horse town,
the fabulous centaur, and goodness, herself.

Communion

When the octopus is wide-eyed, is that innocence?
When he narrows his eyes, is he being discerning?
He is a cold-blooded pioneer who'd approach me
from many angles, he would even change his colour
if the surroundings suggest that he should.
If I were to lift him from his glass tank,
he would pulse with interest, and accommodate
himself into the palm of my hand,
as if he had been born for that purpose.
He reveals as much as does that meteorite
we passed *en route* to the museum, standing
half the height of a man, conserved on a plinth
in the street, worn smooth by our compulsion
to stroke it, and by the atmosphere.

Eye of the hedgehog

Patient in his 'died and gone to heaven' pose,
that berry-eyed glint of such intelligence
is in actual fact a composition involving the mirror image
of two fluorescent striplights, poised to converge,
and a square of window out to Constitution Terrace,
where the roadworks' drilling is threatening to agitate
the boxed moths upstairs from their wings,
to startle, on this level, the doll-like pupil
from where she haunts the centre of the eye
of every once-live thing.